What Can I Touch?

by Sally Wittman
illustrations by Andrea Barrett

Harcourt Brace & Company
Orlando Atlanta Austin Boston San Francisco Chicago Dallas New York Toronto London

Touch the goat.
No. It plays too rough.

Touch this shell.
It's rough to touch.

Touch that.
No! I won't touch that!

This fish isn't rough or tough. Touch it.
I'm not fast enough!

Mine is tough to eat!

Had enough?
More than enough!

A snake can slough off its skin.
Yuck!

I won't touch a sloughing snake!

I've had enough of rough, tough, and slough! What can I touch?

I'll touch you! You're not sloughing your skin. You're not rough. You're fun to touch.

Its kiss feels rough!
Yuck!